De

DARE
2
DREAM

Pushing Past Your Pain to Pursue Purpose

Dream Big! - Pursue

NICOLE B. SIMPSON

DARE
2
DREAM

Pushing Past Your Pain to Pursue Purpose

Dare 2 Dream
Pushing Past the Pain to Pursue Purpose
Published by: Harvest Wealth Media Group
Second Edition Harvest Wealth LLC
371 Hoes Lane Ste. 200 Piscataway, NJ 08854

Copyright 2009 by Nicole B. Simpson First Printing 2009
First Edition: December 2009
Second Printing 2020
Second Edition: April 2020

Cover Design: View Intelligence Graphics Photography Video
All Scripture quotation translations are specifically identified
This book does not necessarily represent the views of any single person
interviewed in its entirety.

www.nicolebsimpson.com

Telephone: 732-377-2024
Library of Congress Cataloging-in-Publication Data: Simpson, Nicole B, 1971-
Dare 2 Dream/ Nicole B. Simpson,--
ISBN: 978-0-9843654-9-4
Inspirational/Christian Living/Religion

Dedication

To my heavenly Father who is always with me. To every individual who chose to share their dreams with me, and to my family who gives me the freedom to pursue my dreams.

ACKNOWLEDGEMENTS

I would like to take this time out to say thank you to my family- Jesse IV, Emani and my bonus son Ian Duhart. Your love, support and commitment to the ministry assignment God has entrusted to me cannot go unrecognized. I could never pursue such lofty dreams without your permission. Thank you. To Elder Stacey T. Densmore of Community Tabernacle Church because of your obedience to the Lord through the W.O.R.T.H. conference where Dare to Dream was originally birthed. To my spiritual mother Evangelist Beverly Allen, because of your wisdom, guidance, unconditional support and love. To my sister Sonji Grandy who has always invested heavily into all of my dreams, to the women of Edna Mahan Correctional Facility former and presently incarcerated because you serve as the best focus group a dreamer could ever ask for. To my entire New Brunswick Theological Seminary class of 2016 who demand that I dream new dreams and pursue them with great tenacity so that I am not left behind. To Rev. Lewis J. Dixon who has spent many days listening to me dream new dreams. To my family at Micah 7 Ministries-special thanks to my entire leadership team. Finally, I want to extend a very special thank you to every individual who helped make my original publication of Dare 2 Dream a great success. I pray that your support and reverence toward me and my dreams will ignite you to dream new dreams.

TABLE OF CONTENTS

PROLOGUE

If you asked me would the day arrive that I would consider revising Dare to Dream, I would have responded with an emphatic "no!" In my mind, it was a moment in time reflection, my sentiments after a very dark season in my life, a season where I was being challenged to dream when I felt that my dreams were dead. But what a difference a decade makes. In ten short years, I managed to accomplish significant milestones, cumulating with the official titled Dr. Nicole B. Simpson, CFP®. Ten years ago, I had not yet completed my Bachelor of Science degree.

So why are we here? As we were approaching the turn of a new decade, the universal thought for many individuals included accomplishing new goals, dreaming new dreams, envisioning life more broadly from a positive and encouraging perspective. People were fully committed to pursuing their destiny. Then the entire world stood still. In a matter of days, a pandemic that originated out of Wuhan China brought the world to a screeching halt. Life has literally slowed down, and we have been forced to restrict our physical movements. Panic began to creep in and even now, the ability to dream has been difficult at best. How does one dream when it feels like your life is falling apart? In the midst of my despair, I figured it out. Now, allow me to provide the additional insight I have learned over the last ten years. Now more than ever, I believe this one book can really change a person's destiny. It could have a profound effect so that you will actually begin to think differently. So, I am honored to help you navigate through these tumultuous times and still realize your dreams.

If by chance you find yourself reading this book, I know in my heart that it's because you are at a place in your life where you're ready to resurrect your dreams. Perhaps you are thinking about your future in a way you never have before and are prepared to step out on faith and bring substance to your dreams.

My prayer is that your creativity explodes with the turning of each page and flows flow like a gentle stream on a beautiful spring morning. By the time you reach the end of this book. My expectation is that you will be bursting with creativity that soars like the waves of a great hurricane.

Within the depths of your soul is a door desperately waiting to be unlocked—a door that has been blocked by indecisiveness, apprehension, and fear. And tucked away behind that door are your dreams, your heart desires, and more importantly, your purpose.

Until now, you've been searching frantically for the key that will unlock the innermost secrets you've housed for years—one that will unlock all of the clutter, all of the pain and all of the baggage that has hindered and separated you from your dreams, but things are about to change. Today is a new day!

If you desire, and I know you do, you can put the past behind you right now and press forward into the future you've always dreamed of. However, as you move boldly toward that door, I ask that you always remember that fear is the absolute greatest hindrance to your success.

Fear of being mocked, or laughed at destroys people's audacity to dream. Of course, no one wants to be laughed at, but unfortunately, it's a part of life that we must deal with and overcome. However, if you open your heart to what I am going to share with you, I promise that by the end of this journey, you will be liberated from all dream-killing hindrances. You will be refreshed and renewed in your spirit. In essence, you will be free to DARE to DREAM again!

DEAD DREAMS

Death is an inevitable and unavoidable part of life, and when a person passes their life literally becomes an open book for all to read. People usually gather to mourn and comfort the survivors, and it's during those moments that family and friends share stories about the deceased; sometimes jokingly and sometimes in a serious manner.

These times can be quite special. Nevertheless, after the funeral, or memorial service, the deceased's body is taken to the cemetery where it, along with the dreams it once housed, will be buried for eternity.

I am overwhelmed with grief every time I visit a cemetery. More than the grief of physical death, I am most impacted by the fact that cemeteries are full of songs that will never be produced or sung and books that will never be written, or turned into plays and Broadway productions. Housed in linen-lined coffins are creative ideas and witty inventions that will never come to fruition and businesses that could have likely employed thousands of people. Yet those dreams will never see the light of day!

I hate to think about all the dreams that died with someone's last breath. What's worse is that most, if not all, people who've died often had every intention of accomplishing their dreams. They were going to get around to it one day, but they never found the time, didn't have the money, or were too distracted by the issues of life. Many were so busy trying to survive and maintain their sanity that they never even gave themselves permission to focus on something abstract. Consequently, they wound up living a life of mediocrity and dying long before their dreams were fulfilled.

The new decade has extended society at large an olive branch. We have all been granted a chance to sit down and critically reflect upon our goals, dreams, and true aspirations. Death has been prevalent. People have succumbed to the virus of COVID 19 in epic proportions, causing many people to ponder the true value of life. It has caused people to contemplate the fact that many are here today and gone tonight. Have you made an indelible mark on society? Have you contributed substantively to your family legacy in a manner that will cause your family members to share your historical contributions to the next generation of your specific clan? Ask yourself, do I want to be the person others say could've done more with their life? Do I want my memory to be characterized with could of, should of, would of's?

If the answer is no, I have great news for you—you are still breathing, which means it's not too late. You can still achieve your dreams. You are in your right mind and the choice to succeed is yours, but you have to first decide if you will continue living a life that is dictated by your circumstances or begin to proactively pursue your dreams.

Unless you are totally fulfilled in every area of your life, you still have desires and things you must accomplish. You may even have some desires that you have kept secret for a long time and never shared them with anyone else, but they're still there. An example of what I mean can best be expressed by my desire to be on Wheel of Fortune. Every time I watch the show, I literally envision myself as a contestant. I've even got a fool-proof strategy that will undoubtedly guarantee I will not go home empty-handed. I know exactly what I would say to Pat Sajak and Vanna White.

Even though I have this strong desire, I've never even attempted to find out the rules and regulations for being a contestant. Honestly, the fear of rejection or the thought that it's impossible for me has caused me to take myself out of the contest before I even submitted my name. Sadly, the same thing happens to people every day; but I am writing this book to ensure that it never happens to you, or me again.

A more pressing objective was to acquire my college degree. As a young teenage mom, an unanticipated pregnancy changed the trajectory of my life. While I managed to land on my feet while pursuing a career in the securities industry, I still had a desire to graduate college to both honor my mother and set a standard for my children. It was a goal I was actively pursuing when I released the first version of this book. In December 2013, my dream was fulfilled. I graduated from Oral Roberts University with honors. I started taking two classes each semester at a local bible college who had a credit for credit partnership which I took full advantage of when I completed half of the graduation prerequisites for the university. It took me an additional two years and a full college schedule, but that was the first dream I fulfilled during the last decade.

Now, what are you prepared to do? Are you going to stand on the sidelines of life afraid to participate? Or are you going to fight for what you desire and begin pursuing your dreams one step at a time? Generally, when I ask this question, the pushback that I get is based on people who do not know how to tackle their dreams, or how to get started. So, I want to encourage you to consider this, "What one thing of interest keeps showing up in my life?" That is the perfect place to start.

Dead Dreams

When you look back over your life, what is the one dream that you want to be able to say became a reality in your life?

_____

_____

_____

_____

What attention have you given to that dream? What research did you do to determine if your dream has the remote possibility of becoming a reality?

_____

_____

_____

_____

Dare 2 Dream

Create a checklist. Today I am going to pursue my dreams. My first three steps are listed below.

1._____

_____

2._____

_____

3._____

_____

INNOCENT DREAMS

Think for a moment and fill in the blank. As a young girl, or boy playing with your toys, whether it was a doll or a truck, you must have thought, When I grow up, I want to _____."

The innocence of childhood is so invigorating. If you were anything like me, your imagination wandered down so many different paths—from thinking about your family to how many children you would have, or even about your future husband, or wife. You might have even been the love-struck child who drew hearts on notebooks with the names of your secret crushes in a heart. Do you remember how vivid, detailed, and full of adjectives your plans for the future would be?

When children are young, they think can be the best at whatever it is they desire to accomplish. I wanted to be famous; I was going to be a superstar. I always imagined my name in lights blazing on billboards as millions of people came to see me. I could literally see the bright lights and hear the crowds chanting my name; however, I never even thought about singing, dancing, or acting. If anything, I wanted to be a track star or a basketball player.

If you think about it, you can probably remember what captured your attention at that age and began to interest you more than anything in the world. I'd be more than willing to bet that your connection to it was innocent, filled with naivety, and a sense of pureness that can never be recaptured. That was an innocent dream.

I remember a little boy in our neighborhood who used to stand on the street curb watching the cars whiz down the block. He was a fixture in my community. He was so intrigued by the different shapes, colors, and speeds of cars that he even learned about the different companies and their flagship models. Even now, I sometimes think that his love and passion for cars at such a young age should have been nurtured and cultivated. I can't help but wonder where he would be had his parents encouraged him to pursue his interests. He could've likely become the next product designer of your favorite automobile. He could've been an executive at Ford, Chrysler, or General Motors, or the visionary behind solar-powered, or battery-operated vehicles; but we will never know now!

Think about a friend you had growing up who always wanted to take care of you. They always wanted to play house, cook food, or be the doctor, or the nurse. Just think, if nurtured, their natural ability could've opened doors in a field of nursing, or social work.

Everyone remembers growing up with a kid who never wanted to get their clothes dirty. They loved to play dress up, match colors and fabrics, and perhaps drew a lot using an array of beautiful patterns. These are the children that likely had a wonderful eye for design.

Consequently, having the ability to earn money doing what they love to do would have been a perfect fit for them.

Finally, think about the kid who would never leave the kitchen. They always wanted to help cook and didn't even mind cleaning up because they understood it was part of preparing the meal. These are the people who would get excited when their mom, or dad would let them crack eggs, fetch the butter, or stir a pot. Then, once the meal was complete, they would be so proud to tell everyone that they helped cook and would recount their participation in preparing the meal over and over again.

All of these examples are about kids dreaming about their future and tapping into the possibilities that lie ahead. Sure, they may not verbalize their desire to work at all, let alone in any particular field; however, you'll see these children gravitating toward the things they love to do. These kids all have something in common. They probably never thought about doing what they love to do for a living because it came so naturally. As a matter of fact, for them, success is virtually inevitable. Failure is not even an option!

So, when is the turning point in a child's life—the point when they are first introduced to the reality of failure? When are they introduced to no, don't, can't and impossible? When does failure become real? Upon reflection, I recognized that I correlated innocent dreams with youth and pondered the origin of that notion. I realized the level of innocence associated with being young and oblivious to failure provides you with a broader lens to see life optimistically. That reality for me made me consider ways to recapture the freedom connected to dreaming big dreams uninhibited. I came up with an exercise that allows your thoughts to wander freely without interruption or invisible barriers. It requires work on your behalf, but I believe once you begin, you will feel liberated.

This is designed for people who desire to dictate the outcome of their future instead of allowing their circumstances to define their successes or failures in life. You have to desire more than what society expects from you. You have dreams, goals, desires, and a gift that can help you accomplish everything you seek to achieve. So, grab a pen and get a notebook. Take a moment to select a song that calms you, allows you to slow down and relax. Put that song on repeat until you have cleared your mind. You have the opportunity to approach your writing time in several ways. I suggest you begin with a concrete thought and a set time. That means, you literally say, "I am going to write about my dream house for 15 minutes.", or you can consider, "I am going to write about the wind for five minutes." You have no boundaries, you set the objective...and the timer! Now you are ready to write.

Free based writing is a wonderful technique that allows you to declutter what is in your mind because it allows you to write without being inhibited. There is no focus on grammar, continuity, or complete thoughts. You have the space to write single words, whole sentences, or fractured thoughts. I have found it to be invaluable while attempting to process the myriad of emotions I experienced after having to face the fact that I was traumatized by my World Trade Center experience. Before you think you may have missed something, you didn't. I will elaborate further in the next chapter. But free based writing was one of the techniques I used to identify and ultimately process those emotions.

The ability to write out how I feel-my anger, fears, worries, frustrations, and anxieties- was a lifesaver because I was too afraid to articulate them verbally for fear that I might be giving life to my struggles. While it took some time, I eventually began to dream again. It was slow. The process was painful at times, but it also allowed me to recapture the innocence of my youth. I was able to write about what life would have been like had I not experienced such trauma.

When you give yourself permission to get lost in a dream, you recapture the innocence of your youth. It takes you to the place of invincibility. In your dreams, you can overcome anything, conquer the world, defeat the largest giant. I humbly submit that if you can dream it if you can see yourself in that space, those innocent dreams have the potential of becoming a reality.

What song helps you to clear your mind?

_____

Write, write, write!

_____

_____

_____

_____

_____

_____

_____

Ask yourself, what am I good at?

_____

_____

_____

_____

Does this ability come to me naturally? □ Yes□ No

If I had my choice, what would I do with my life?

_____

_____

_____

_____

Compare your talent with your desire. Are they similar? How do they differ?

_____

_____

_____

_____

III

SHATTERED

A little boy, six-years-old, falls off the merry-go-round and begins to cry. His initial instinct is to find his mommy because he knows she will make everything better. He finds her sitting with other people and immediately runs into her arms, but instead of being met with a warm, comforting embrace, he's confronted with a cold, unemotional voice that says, "Quit crying and stop acting like a sissy! Little boys don't cry."

Sadly, this was not an uncommon scenario for the boy. In his heart, he hoped this time would be different. He hoped that this time his mommy would respond like mommies should, with concern, love, and compassion.

Have you ever been rejected by your parents? Do you know how it feels to have a mom, or dad prefer drugs and alcohol over you? Imagine not having a parent to guide you through the complexities of life. Imagine having no one to help you with your homework, fix you breakfast, or dinner. Even worse, imagine if when you did see mom, she was always yelling, screaming, and oftentimes using you as a human punching bag? What if you had sisters and brothers and because you were the oldest child you had to become a surrogate parent to them, even though you were only three, or four years older than they were? Yet you know that if you didn't do it, no one else would. While you're picturing this scenario, imagine if you were expected to go to school, get good grades, and then come home and care for your siblings. Although these scenarios may be hard to visualize, this lifestyle is a reality for many. People who often ask themselves if this is all life has to offer.

"You're stupid! You will never amount to anything! You're just like your father! You're a whore, slut, sissy, crybaby!"

Life can become truly unbearable when the very people who are supposed to love you continue to call you out of your name; especially if it's your mom, dad, grandma, or granddad. You might figure they should know; however, after hearing you will never amount to anything, you'll eventually begin to believe it and stop expecting great things. This is where quite a number of dreams die!

Maybe that's not your story. Perhaps you were minding your business, going to work, and pursuing the American dream. Then one day terrorists decide to attack the building where you were employed, causing deaths too numerous to count, and thousands of people physically affected for years thereafter. On September 11, 2001, America was shattered because that is exactly what happened.

Personally, I worked on the 73rd floor of Two World Trade Center and I was in a meeting when Tower One was hit. Initially, I did not intend to leave the building, but after walking into my partner's office and seeing burning paper floating in the air, my team sought to vacate the premises. Unfortunately, we were still on the 44th floor when Tower Two, the building we were in, was hit as well. Had we not left when we did, we would not have been below the airplane's impact.

The country's security was shattered! Death shattered the lives of families! Survivors lives were shattered! Survivors struggled for years trying to regain a sense of normalcy in their lives, many too little, or no avail. How do you recover from such a devastating hit when life was drastically altered without your participation, or consent? You were dealt a terrible hand in life and expected to recover without support, direction, or any guidance.

The global financial crisis that began in 2007 and really rocked America at the core in 2008 was universally considered one of the worse economic downturns since the Great Depressions. Businesses failed, people lost their life savings and many homes were foreclosed. The stock market plummeted, and it took years for people to recover. Many are still affected at the turn of the century. Shattered!

One final, collective shattering experience impacted the entire world. A virus originated out of Wuhan China named COVID 19 and it has been classified as deadly and extremely contagious. It is a resilient strain that caused a global standstill. Businesses closed, the global market tanked, production ceased, food shortages are in various communities, while the death toll is stubbornly increasing as this book goes to print. The entire health system in America is shattered!

Dream Killers

My first vivid memory is of me at six years old. I can often recall glimpses of my childhood, but one experience I've never forgotten happened the day my mom took my sister to the annual Back-to-School event. It was one of those events where parents met their children's teachers at the beginning of the school year.

Normally, the parents would go alone, unless they had a child who was starting kindergarten. Because my sister was new into the kindergarten class, my mother took her to meet her new teacher, Ms. Budninsky. While they attended the parent-teacher meeting, I was at left home where I was introduced to a man who instructed me to touch, fondle and kiss him in areas I'd known to be "private parts." This continued for seven years, and during that time I learned nearly every way to please a man sexually. I'd had more semen shot into my mouth than I even care to remember. Every day I prayed that each time I was summoned would be the last, but it never was.

Abandonment, sexual assault, molestation, domestic violence, teenage pregnancy, chronic illness, death and so many other unforeseen circumstances are all very traumatic events that introduce young children to mortality. Before these life- changing events most children feel invincible—never understanding the meaning of failure. That is, until they are introduced to it by some person or circumstance. These people and experiences are what I refer to as dream killers!

The aftermath of these memories and experiences are often so great, so overwhelming that they have the potential to dictate the course of our lives. What's worse is that when we refuse to face them head on, acknowledge their power and impact over our past, we become destined to repeat history and allow those memories to infect our future just as they have our past. As a result, the decisions and choices we make will likely be based in fear, not faith. Then, it is likely that we will replace positive thinking with an expectation of mediocrity. This is the precise point when people begin to react negatively.

Instead of responding proactively and taking control of their lives, they position themselves to be a victim of their circumstances— waiting for life to come to them instead of going out to conquer the world through the power of their dreams.

My personal experience is just that. People who identify with my story must find the inner strength to combat their stories so they can overcome those traumatic experiences that have kept them limited in their ability to not only dream, but to also find the energy to pursue those dreams. This is critical to know unsolicited help is not coming. When you change your mindset that you will not allow your past to dictate your destiny, it feels as if the shift of that mindset invites support that will allow you to successfully confront your past and defeat its grip on your future. Universal dream killers are like giants who appear to have the upper hand. At first glance, it appeared that David would be naturally crushed by Goliath because he was a mere lad and Goliath was a great warrior. When the financial infrastructure was shattered to no fault of the average American working hard daily trying to provide for their family, the ability to recover was not solely based on individual resilience and tenacity, but also required government intervention. That intervention was disparate in that the wealthy recovered and those in poverty are still struggling over a decade later.

We are experiencing the disproportionate intervention once again as we deal with the pandemic COVID 19. What originated as a health crisis, spilled into an economic tsunami washing away the minimal assets of middle America. In addition to minorities and the elderly population dying in significant numbers because the healthcare system has been sub-par for many generations leading up to this moment, the spotlight is finally on such an atrocity. Dreams are dying daily.

If you don't push to keep the childlike dream in you alive, you'll discover that as days become weeks and the weeks become years, whatever dreams you originally had will became faint, distant memories trapped within the depths of your soul never to see the light of day. I beg you not to let this be your story.

What painful childhood experiences still affect the decisions you make today?

_____

_____

_____

_____

_____

What are some of the negative statements you heard in the past that you have internalized? Be honest with yourself. Remember, the only way you can overcome the hurdles before you is to acknowledge your innermost fears and plow through them.

_____

_____

_____

_____

Take this time to reflect on some past mistakes you have made. After all, denying your past isn't going to assist you in changing your future.

_____

_____

_____

_____

_____

How did the tragedy of September 11, 2001 impact your lifestyle?

_____

_____

_____

_____

How did the global economic crisis of 2007-2008 impact your lifestyle?

_____

_____

_____

_____

_____

How did the health crisis COVID 19 impact your lifestyle?

_____

_____

_____

_____

Need more space?

_____

_____

_____

_____

_____

_____

In spite of all of that, guess what? You're still standing. Even if you're hanging by a thread, or by the skin of your teeth, your past did not kill you. You may feel dead emotionally, but as long as you still have a pulse and the strength to exist from moment to moment and day to day, you have something you can work with.

DARE TO DREAM

Have you ever had a dream that seemed so real you actually thought you were awake? What about the dream that ended abruptly before you reached the climax? If it was a good dream, you probably wanted to hurry up and get back to sleep so you could enjoy the conclusion., or you were actually upset when the alarm clock went off, someone turned on the light, or the telephone rang. However, if you're having a nightmare, a wave of gratitude overshadows you when someone saves you from getting stabbed, shot, or hurt in any way.

When you're having a bad dream, right before the impact of devastation you usually wake up in a cold sweat, shaking and breathing heavily. Many kids wet the bed because of the fear of the boggy man, bad dreams, or experiences they could never talk about while awake so they play out their emotions in their dreams.

Now, I'm no expert or psychiatrist, but after living life in fear of the outcome of my nightmares, I decided to take matters in my own hand. For example, if I was losing a fight, I'd will myself to stay asleep until I came out victorious. That's my competitive nature. I don't like in losing, even in a dream. Truthfully speaking, I cannot determine the legitimacy of my feelings, but emotionally, it's important for me to maintain control at all times. I know I have the power to dictate the outcome of my dreams. I have the ability to write my journey, even in my subconscious state. I have purposed to take control over all of my successes and failures, even when someone violates, or takes advantage me and tries to kill my spirit. I'm in control, and I, not any other human being, have the power over me.

A decade later, such notions seem so naïve simply because I've experienced more nightmares than I care to recount. The subconscious state was far more powerful than will or resolve. The nightmares caused me to lose thousands of hours of rest. In addition, I realized I only addressed lucid dreams, the ones you have the power to control the outcome. The nightmares were shaped because of the multiple crisis experiences I endured which were saturated in trauma, causing additional stress and anxiety.

Dreams and visions are the gateway to the inner world—a world that is even more real than this physical world. Dream analysis informs us in visual language about repressed experiences and other processes of our unconscious. The more applicable definition of dream is a desired ambition, desire, or goal. That is controllable, achievable and something one can build upon.

The Dare!

A dare is defined as a challenge to do something risky. So how does one dare to dream? By evaluating their repressed experiences and challenges in a manner that produces a different outcome in the realm of reality. You can dare to dream by facing all of your traumatic experiences, acknowledging their impact and moving forward in spite of whatever injuries, or pain you've suffered.

I know you can do this. You are not weak, or stupid. You've survived until this point because the fighter in you will not allow you to give up, cave in and quit. Sure, it may feel like you're in the final three minutes of the twelfth round of a grueling boxing match, but I have great news for you—the fight is fixed and you win! The only thing you need to do is believe and operate as if the fight just started.

I must caution you that this is not going to be easy. I don't want to mislead anyone into believing that in a matter of days, weeks, or month's positive thinking will erase years of abuse and abandonment; because it won't. Neither will it bring back a deceased loved one, or make a chronic illness disappear. You will still experience pain and it is likely that you will still cry when something familiar triggers a memory. However, make sure that you do not put a period where God has placed a comma. What I mean is it's not over yet. Your destiny is not finalized. If it were, you'd be dead. As long as you have breath in your body, you have an opportunity to change, grow and dream.

One additional thought is imperative to state. The turn of the 21st century has added multiple layers of complexities that need to be considered in the equation. From the tragedy of September 11th to the global economic crisis of 2007-2008 to the current pandemic COVID 19. It feels like each time an individual gains ground and recovers from the uncontrolled, devastating blows we have endured as Americans, something new happens. The security of America, the financial stability and now the physical health and overall well-being. This is not fathom. The impact or results are real. You can dare to dream and outside conditions fight you every step of the way. But quitting, or tapping out is not an option. You absolutely cannot give up on...you!

Are you satisfied with where you are in life? What changes, big, or small, can you make that will improve your quality of life?

_____

_____

_____

_____

Dear to Dream!

Throughout this chapter, you have been thinking about the different experiences in your past, particularly the most difficult and challenging ones. Now I want you to reflect on the positive memories. What moments bring a smile to your face? Where were you and what were you doing? Who were the people around you?

_____

_____

_____

_____

What dare, what challenges did you accept in the past? Reflect upon your decision to take a risk in that area. What was the outcome? Did you achieve the desired results?

_____

_____

_____

_____

BACK TO BASICS

If we couldn't dream, our lives wouldn't mean anything anymore.

GEORGE KAISER

What a powerful statement! You don't have to exist without meaning and without a purpose. Yet and still, most people cannot even identify their true purpose.

Your purpose is the reason you exist. It's specifically what were you placed on this Earth to accomplish.

God declared that He formed you before the foundation of the world and that He has a plan and purpose for your life. However, the only way you can identify your true purpose in life is to go back to the basics. I believe exploring your natural gifts, talents, and abilities will provide you with the answers you're so desperately seeking. Now that I am a little wiser with age and experience, I have determined that you may also find your purpose was birthed out of experiences you had throughout life. For example, a child who experienced seasons of homelessness may focus on providing shelter for children on the street. If someone experienced serious bouts of hunger, they may work to ensure everyone hungry in a particular area can get a meal. It doesn't have to be negative. Singing, or dancing, or bowling may have been your love, or passion growing up and you want others to experience a comparable joy.

The point is that going back to the basics is taking a moment to find the organic, life-altering moments that defined your way of existence. The influence can be both positive and negative. It is what gives you the ammunition to fight another day. It checks a primary invisible box to the question asked, "If money were not an issue, what would you do with your life?"

I am convinced that the reason people stray so far away from the basics is because they have allowed people to negatively influence them. You know, the people who tell you to grow up and let go of the past. The ones with whom you've shared your innermost thoughts, and they just rejected them and told you to stop dreaming and get real. Adding insult to injury, they say things like, "You will never amount to anything. That's not a great business plan. You don't have enough money. That's not going to feed your family."

If you allow it, those negative statements can weigh heavily on your emotions and impact the decisions you make. However, during your period of reflection, I am certain you identified some natural gifts you noticed budding in you even in your youth; things that you've never given up on in spite of what others said. It is that very passionate resolve that will carry you through the times when it seems like no one is supporting you.

We are all blessed with at least one superior gift. Some of us have multiple gifts and abilities but know with surety that each of us has at least one gift. Through it, we have the opportunity to excel, shine, and truly make a significant difference in this world. So where are you standing now? Are you working a traditional nine to five begging for overtime because you need extra money just to maintain a mediocre standard of living? This is a secondary reason why people stray away from the basic. It is out of sheer necessity, oftentimes because you have economic responsibilities that require you to exchange your time for a set amount of money each hour. Pursuing your purpose has a price tag too high for you to consider in the moment. So that traditional nine to five, even with the extra hours, has you barely making ends meet and still living from paycheck to paycheck.

Here is the kicker—are you even happy?
Are you spending the majority of your day working and doing something that's totally unfulfilling and unproductive? Who wants to live like that?

Sadly, this is the reality for so many people. This is why discovering your purpose is so important. When you know your purpose, your circumstances could remain the same, but in due season, the change will eventually occur. Why? Because when you are giving your purpose some of your time, you'd be fulfilled and personally content with where you were and what you were doing. Imagine getting to a point of loving what you do to such a degree that you are willing to come into the office on your days off. A place where, if you could, you would spend all of your free time focused on your work; and if possible, do it for free.

I strongly believe that contentment makes you strive toward perfection. If you're content in your job, you'd look for ways to excel in that field, and your willingness toward being the best would ensure your temporary circumstances were destined to change. How, you might ask? How does one turn something good into something great? Through practice, commitment, education, and discipline; that's how! When you find something you love, when you find your purpose, you'll be able to identify your calling and your gift and embrace everything that comes along with it. Let me give you an illustration. Originally, I thought I was destined to be an attorney or a politician. I worked hard to get good grades in school so that I could get a scholarship and all of my hard work paid off. However, I got pregnant the summer before I was to begin Seton Hall University. Now, I know there are people who would've still gone to college and made it work; but I chose to put school on hold so I could get a job and care for my son.

At that point in time, I deferred the opportunity to go to school on scholarship and got a job instead. There were plenty of people who said I'd blown it and that my life was over. They said I was wasted potential, but I disagreed. In retrospect, I now see how it was actually one of the best things that could've ever happened to me.

It took me four months of working at a mediocre job to realize I would not survive operating the same way for the remainder of my life. The first time I was due for a raise months later, it was for $.50 cents. So, I immediately began looking for a job that would upgrade me more than $.50 measly cents hour each year.

During one of the job interviews, I was exposed to the possibility of working on Wall Street. The interview turned out to be with a school that virtually guaranteed its student's job placement in the financial services industry. I loved math and working with people seemed possible, so I gave it a shot.

I had quit my job to attend school and after six weeks I was considering dropping out. Although I loved what I was learning, the mounting mound of bills made me think I'd made the worst decision of my life. However, one of my teacher's saw something in me he'd never seen in another student...so he said. He mentioned a program that helped people on welfare and unemployment go to school; however, I couldn't get any support since I wasn't on welfare and quit my job.

With things looking nearly impossible, the teacher asked me how much money I needed every week in order to stay in school. I averaged out my expenses and determined I needed at least $80 per week for pampers and formula. He offered to pay me that amount out of his own pocket and promised me I'd be the first student he sent on an interview. That's how much he believed in me!

Six weeks later, I went on my first job interview at Prudential Bache and got a temporary job as a bond counter that paid me more in one day than my teacher gave me for an entire month.

After working for Prudential Bache part-time for two months, I was offered a full-time position that paid $20,000 a year. That was in 1991. I was 20 years, didn't have a college degree, and in less than a year wound up making a pretty decent living. Life was good; and only getting better!

My teacher, who had become my mentor, then instructed me

take my Series 7 exam to become licensed in the field as soon as I got my foot in the door. Initially, I wasn't embraced by the people I worked with. I was the only minority working in midtown New York on Madison Avenue in the Revlon building. Just the same, within my first year on the job, I copied the materials to study from a friend. Since my position really did not demand the license, when I was ready, I negotiated an agreement with the company and agreed to pay for my sponsorship if I failed my exam.

I studied at home with the help of my boyfriend-turned- husband after work every day for eight months. I passed the test the first time and was on my way. I was determined to succeed because I'd found something I loved to do and was good at.

Within five years, I literally doubled my annual income and became licensed in several different financial areas. My goal at the time was to become a Certified Financial Planner®. Yes me, the sexual abused, teenage mother and college drop out from the projects had actually made it! That's when I began to harness my potential to change the world around me.

My love for financial planning in itself is not my purpose. However, it's in line with what I am truly called to do. I will elaborate on that later.

I have a friend who was extremely successful in the corporate world. However, she was not happy. As a salesperson, she hit all her target numbers, went on tons of the fancy trips and met all of the company's sales goals. She was compensated well and worked hard to achieve that level of success, but still struggled internally. Success in tow, there was still something missing from my friend's life. Consequently, she continually sought after a high that could not be achieved. Knowing that she loved working with people more than numbers, she eventually switched careers. Once again, success found her, but the same emptiness persisted.

Most people will settle for less if the price is right. Unfortunately, that's because we are extremely short-sighted when it comes to understanding the true meaning of success. Here is what I observed about my friend: she loved to teach. If she worked on a project with you, she'd put together a curriculum before you even began. She'd account for every aspect of the event, complete with pre and post planning. She could've easily been an event planner, but teaching was her strength. She has the unique ability to break down something extremely complicated into a "Do's for dummies." She can listen to your objectives and in no time flat provide you with a plan that includes a methodology, resources and a line item budget.

In my heart, I always knew she was born to teach. For years I watched her struggle with God about her career because she didn't consider teaching a financially lucrative career choice. However, when things went from bad to worse, she finally surrendered.

The moment she embraced teaching something phenomenal happened. We were in the midst of the worse recession of our lifetime, yet she was getting interviews and offers for teaching jobs too numerous to count. Additionally, she was engulfed with peace that money could never buy. Today, she is teaching, but most importantly, she has the time she needs for her children and the time to sow into the lives of other children as well.

What am I saying? If you're going to work hard just to survive, at least do what you love to do. Well that sounds beautiful Nicole, you might say, but how do I do that? I'm glad you asked.

DREAMING WITH YOUR GIFT IN MIND

Transition is never easy. People don't like change. Of course, we like to complain about the way things are, but taking the necessary measures to make things different is not something we're easily inclined to do.

There are some people who are legitimately stuck in the midst of their trauma. For example, someone on Dialysis three times a week may have a difficult time pursuing a job that considers their need for a flexible work schedule. You also have moms with small children who are working double shifts to put food on the table, clothes on the kid's backs and keep a roof over their heads. Even though these are some very tough choices to make it is important to be mindful that sometimes the decisions we make are not always the most reasonable ones. For example, let's suppose you are a single parent who is working at Walmart. You were just released from your shift, which should've been eight hours, but it turned into eleven hours because someone didn't show up for work. You stayed because you needed the overtime. Of course, you're extremely tired by the time you get off and the thought of going home to cook a meal sounds exhausting. So, you decide to pick up a pizza or stop by the drive-thru at McDonalds. Of course, the $10 you spent doesn't seem like a lot; however, if you did that four times a month, you would've spent $40. You may be thinking, Well what's the big deal? The big deal is that small expenditures like those add up quickly and are the main reason people remain impoverished.

If we fail to operate in wisdom where our finances are concerned, little expenditures like hair, nails, snacks at work and lunch money for the kids can very easily cancel out any overtime we work.

Here is where the investment into yourself will begin to make sense. Take the same scenario, but instead of working overtime, you decide to go to school to pursue your passion. Bear in mind that because you have three small children and limited earnings, you will be a viable candidate for grants, not loans.

In this scenario, the sacrifice of your time would be a solid investment into your future. You may have to shop with coupons, cook every night, and pinch penny's like never before. However, you'd be doing so with a definite end in sight; and it wouldn't be very long before you eventually finished school. Most importantly, you'd be working toward your dreams. Let me tell you how I know it's possible. Because this is the road I traveled since the concept of Dare to Dream was envisioned.

In the year 2007, I was seriously depressed. Physically my body was not cooperating as my breathing became tedious as I attempted to even walk down a flight of steps, or down a block. I felt like an elephant resided on my chest. I was still struggling financially due to the impact of September 11th, 2001. I worked for commission and was barely making ends meet. It was a catch 22. I could not work because I could not breathe and when I worked, my breathing worsened. At the same time, I was preaching and teaching and making attempts to do whatever possible to survive.

Several years prior, I made the decision to pursue my college degree. I was ready to leave the securities industry and it appeared that I was called into ministry full time. In my industry, bankruptcy is a potential death sentence for a financial planning practitioner. Add to that, the fact that I was a Certified Financial Planner® professional, I felt cornered. Upon reflection, I was hedging my bets, not certain how my life would eventually unfold. I was existing from moment to moment, trying to keep my head above water.

That feeling is an identifiable feeling. Many people understand trying to survive when life is getting the best of you and you're trying to maintain your sanity. It was during this low point of my life, while I was putting one foot in front of the other to exist, the Lord tells me that my dreams were not impressive...literally. I was leading a prayer one evening and I felt the shift in the prayer and the words spilled out of my mouth. "Nicole, your dreams don't impress me. Don't you know I am God!" Wow! What was I supposed to do with that information?

In tough economic times, many people are released from their jobs in cost-cutting efforts. Some have been on their jobs for more than thirty years, and for them, their company was the center of their existence. They were content working every day but in one moment everything was taken away and they were left with nothing. Like many, they made the common mistake of assuming their job would always be there. They became comfortable, never thinking that one day it would all be over. What's worse is that many people in those situations are not mentally, or financially prepared for these types of situations. So, what happens to the once complacent person who's had the rug pulled from under them?

They may struggle with thoughts that no one will hire them simply because of their advanced age and salary requirements. Add to that the fact that they've been in the same field for over thirty years and never got around to getting a college degree and they're facing some hurdles; but nothing that cannot be overcome. I felt secure with my CFP® designation, but my options felt limited to an industry; an industry that would only allow me to earn a living in sales. Well, that would be virtually impossible if I can't walk down a block without feeling as if I were going to pass out. Limited income meant limited co-payments to keep going to the doctors to see what was wrong.

Let me be clear. While I had begun to acquire my college degree, I'm not certain if I changed anything drastically based on my own volition. A series of unanticipated events outside of my control disrupted my life in the most positive way imaginable. (That story is fully addressed in my release Listen and Learn How God Speaks to You). It took me on a pathway that caused me to clean up my credit that had been damaged post 9/11. I established my own financial planning firm and found free, lifetime medical support for World Trade Center survivors. My role in charting the new trajectory of my life was based on my unwavering commitment to make lemonade...no matter what.

It's never too late to begin working on your dreams. We are all ordinary individuals with the potential to achieve extraordinary success. Once we identify our special gifts and abilities and determine how to best nurture them, our potential for success becomes limitless.

This is the point where we can then examine potential career choices that will allow our gifts to blossom to their fullest potential with the option of creating a business for ourselves if we desire. Perhaps you've already identified your passion. You already know you can sing, dance, or recite spoken word. Maybe you can cook, take care of animals, or clean house like grandma used to back in the day. Now, the next thing to ask yourself is, where does my business strength lie? Have you ever created an ultimate plan for your life? If not, there's no time like the present.

I'm challenging you to think outside the box. If money were not an issue, what would you do with your life?

_____

_____

_____

_____

Oftentimes, what you are good at and what you love to do are one and the same. I am encouraging you to begin to evaluate your ability to impact your household, your neighborhood, your state, and the world. Use the examples above as a base and allow them to trigger ideas.

Let me leave you with this promise: when you begin to nurture your God-ordained gift, major opportunities will follow. The question then becomes, will you recognize the open door? As stated above, my decision to make lemonade with what life dealt me created opportunities that I was able to recognize. Therefore, every step I made was a calculated risk that paid off.

Finally, consider this: my decision to leave school ultimately prepared me for a career in the securities industry. In the same vein, God sent an angel in the form of my teacher to walk beside me in my journey of faith. Ultimately, it was not about my teacher, it was about me lining up with the will of God for my life. However, if I never shared my dilemma with my teacher and had instead simply dropped out as I intended, he would've never been able to bless and walk alongside me during my journey.

What is most beautiful is that when the chance to return to school presented itself, I was still capable of fulfilling my dream of becoming a college graduate. I did not become an attorney or a politician, but that was because I thought my natural gifts and talents would be best utilized in those fields. However, when I expanded my worldview, I realized I was skilled, or naturally gifted to flourish in multiple career fields.

What career areas do you believe your gifts can be best utilized?

_____

_____

_____

_____

_____

DREAMS ARE BIGGER THAN YOU

Then the LORD answered me, "Write the vision. Make it clear on tablets so that anyone can read it quickly. The vision will still happen at the appointed time. It hurries toward its goal. It won't be a lie. If it's delayed, wait for it. It will certainly happen. It won't be late.

Habakkuk 2:2-3, GWT

This passage of scripture really speaks to me. It talks about writing down your dreams, not for your personal benefit, but for others to see. I know you're probably thinking, you want me to share my innermost thoughts with other people? Don't worry, this was scary for me too, but the results were well worth it. So now that you've identified your ability and created a plan of action for your life, this is the next step toward progress. As you move forward, I guarantee you will find that this is both personally fulfilling and exciting. At the same time, this may also cause apprehension for some.

My first experience sharing my dreams with others began when I was very young. It worked out well.

I especially understood the value of sharing my dreams with others after publishing my first book, Planning for a Reason, a Season, and a Lifetime. I'd sold all the original copies of the book and was considering writing a second edition.

I was grateful for the success I had with my first book; however, I knew I hadn't taken advantage of every available option to ensure that people were aware of disaster planning. To encourage myself, I visited the women at Edna Mahan Women's Correctional Facility and shared my story with them complete with my book's success and failures. It was a very rough time for me, but I found that in speaking to the young ladies about overcoming their fears, I was able to push past my own fears and move forward with publishing the second edition of my book.

In all honestly, I thought my first book would be on the New York Times bestseller's list. I thought I'd sell millions of books, but I didn't. Still, I couldn't shake the feeling that I had more to accomplish. So, I went back to the drawing board. This time I shared my dreams with other people. You see, I had accomplished a great deal and was independently successful the first time based on my own skills. However, when I shared my vision with other people, they began to add to and enhance what God had given me. That is when the miracles began.

Read carefully, because what I'm getting ready to share is the benefit of revising Dare to Dream a decade later. The most valuable lesson I learned in pursuing my dreams is the recognition that your dreams should be bigger than you. You can fulfill a dream alone, but if you have vision, it requires help. What is the difference? I know I have been talking about dreams up to this point. The ability to accomplish a goal, or fulfill an objective is indeed possible. I finished school individually. But why? Because what I thought was my dream, was a small piece of the puzzle to the vision for my life. I was thinking about a plan that required wisdom and imagination.

Have you ever watched the movie The Wiz? Since I was a teenager, and to this present day, the Wiz has been a staple in my life. When one is seeking to fulfill their life purpose, a vision, the plan God has for their life, they need a team. Nestled in the story of The Wiz are the role planners who assist you in fulfilling your destiny. At least it worked for me. You need a Scarecrow, a Lion and a Tin Man. The scarecrow is the intellectual challenger that will help you see varied perspectives when looking to pursue your dream. They may offer advice, draw your attention to pitfalls and vulnerabilities, push you forward with sage words of wisdom. They are smart and they want to see you win.

The Tin Man has the heart. An individual that is extraordinarily kind and compassionate, one that has empathy and the desire to see you excel in life is a perfect addition to the team because they will always find the good in every situation. The most toxic, or devastating of blows in pursuing purpose hurts. The person who validly wants to see you win will feel every emotion with you and find a way out of the darkness to see light. The last team member should be one with courage. They are willing to compel you to take that calculated risk understanding you have more to gain than you have to lose. The Lion in the Wiz felt that he lacked courage, but when it came time to do the hard task, he met that challenge. Building a team ensures a greater probability of success. And if you should be so fortunate to find others who want you to excel in equal measure, well, that enhances your chances to succeed overall.

Sharing your vision with others allows them to assist you in the creative process. I had already identified my gift and wrote the vision, and it never changed, but when I shared my vision with other people, they began to deepen the knowledge God had given me.

Success is a team sport. You will never experience it alone. When we follow our dreams without help, without guidance, and without support, we risk suffering from burn out, which will limit our potential. Too often, we place ourselves in this position, not realizing that it is counterproductive.

When I decided to share the gifts, God had given me with others, the more opportunities began to present themselves. Additionally, people started helping me by sharing their resources and pledging their support of my vision. Of course, I had to allow myself to be vulnerable to criticism, but overall, the feedback was progressive, not regressive.

Certainly, you must be prepared for the dream killers who will not support your vision. However, always remember that although you have the vision, the next step in your journey will almost always be revealed to you by someone else.

Name three people who have supported you unconditionally.

I._____

2._____

3._____

This is a perfect opportunity to call, text, or write the people who support you and are able to stand beside you as you dare to dream. I am certain it will be an ego booster—an encouragement for you and where you are standing today.

Use the space below to begin writing your vision and the dreams God has given you.

_____

_____

_____

_____

Trust your instinct! You are a business and every business must have a team to be successful. I want to share one final example of how important this link is to your overall success. Several years ago, I met a young lady who had recently started a new magazine. She had the desire to become a publisher since she was a little girl, but it wasn't until two close members of her family passed away that she moved forward in her destiny.

When we met, she was at a transition in her life. She had taken the business as far as she could on her own and realized she needed assistance. She had exhausted her options and needed a fresh perspective. She'd shared her vision with women with different levels of expertise and three months later she had a team of people working with her as if the vision was birth by them independently.

If you pray and allow God to order your steps, you will always find yourself traveling in the right direction.

Share the vision!

Reflect upon the three individuals you identified as people who have supported you unconditionally. Do they have the characteristics to be your Wiz team? Write out your thoughts.

_____

_____

_____

VIII

WEATHER THE STORM

The moment you make the decision to follow your dreams, you can almost always expect a major storm to come your way. I don't know what the storm will look like, or how strong it will be, but I do know that it will come. I must add that in life, there are three primary cycles when addressing storms. You are preparing to enter a storm, you are in the midst of one, or you just survived one. The turn of a new decade has placed society at large in the midst of a storm compliments of COVID 19. This isn't simply a storm; it feels like a tornado which is violent and destructive because people are dying in epic numbers too numerous to count. It felt swift and the impact was deadly and we are still in the midst of the cycle of destruction. The thief comes to steal, to kill, and to destroy. But I have come so that you might have life and have it more abundantly, John 10.10

Do you ever wonder why every time things seem to be going well in your life, you become anxious? You begin to wonder when, not if, the shoe is going to drop. This happens mainly because we are naturally pessimistic, but also because the enemy hates when we become determined. So anytime we are committed to living life on purpose, he is coming.

If you believe God and are attempting to line up with his plan for your life, it is the devil's responsibility to act as a roadblock to your success. Recognize that he is on assignment just like you and his objective is to make you fail. And just as God had angels to carry out his plans, Satan also has his evil cronies helping him carry out his. Unfortunately, until you truly depend on God for total instruction and direction, you will fall victim to the traps of the enemy time and time again.

The most invaluable lesson I learned regarding how best to navigate through a vicious storm was simply not to measure my progress, or growth in days, weeks, months, or even years. It released me from the pressure of thinking I would not endure some setbacks and it gave me the liberty to accept a day where I was defeated by the trials of life. Actually, the moment I gave myself permission to fall short occasionally, I found that my days of progress greatly exceeded my days of defeat. You've heard the saying that Rome was not built in a day. Well, pursuing your destiny isn't going to happen overnight. The moment you accept that a major ally in the pursuit of your dreams is time, you will view setbacks from a different perspective. Most people think they cannot handle, or even afford a nonproductive day. Newsflash-you had them, you will continue to have them and they cannot stop you from succeeding. Simply manage them- weather the storm!

This is a perfect time to reflect on the steps you have already taken. Since you've begun this journey, how far have you traveled? What apparent, tangible successes have you achieved?

Savor these milestones as they will serve as an anchor during the storm. In my opinion, this is one area in which the church continues to fail people miserably. Much too often, we don't even discuss the real trials and tribulations people will encounter when they attempt to operate according to the will of God.

Imagine if someone told you that the only way you could ever truly find peace is to accept Jesus as your Lord and personal Savior, but in the same breath, said as a result of accepting Jesus, your life would literally be turned upside down by the devil, who once had you under his control. This is the scenario of the storm—a time when the devil will do everything, he can to convince you to give up on God.

During this time, the devil will point out that the reason why you lost your job, lost your girlfriend and no one loves you is because you're not worthy of their love. He's a liar and he will magnify your trials in an attempt to convince you that God doesn't love you, and he won't stop there! You can surely count on him taking you on a journey of your past and reminding you why you gave up on your dreams in the first place. This is the point in their Christian walk where most people throw in the towel.

For so long the church has been afraid to honestly explore this subject. Instead, the need for Christ in our lives is often portrayed in a disingenuous manner. In an attempt to showcase all that Christ has done for us, the love He has for us and the sacrifice He's made for us, we've not clearly portrayed Christianity. Yes, being in relationship with Christ has priceless benefits, but at the end of the day we all will still be affected by the storms of life.

This book is not intended to convert you to Christianity, but I'd be remiss if I did not share with you the only way that I've been able to survive the many trials and tribulations in my life. The grace and mercy of God have certainly kept me; however, I had to first understand that my relationship with Him would not eliminate pain, but give me the strength to endure it. Likewise, if you hold on to your previous successes, they will give you the courage you need to keep moving and pursuing your dream.

You are a success story! You've overcame seemingly impossible obstacles in the past, and you will overcome whatever roadblocks you're facing now. You can weather the storm, and at the end of it all, you will be stronger, wiser, and capable of helping someone else whether their storm.

IX

DREAMS DO COME TRUE

Dreams are to be pursued in spite of the roadblocks before you. A great example of this is expressed in *'The Pursuit of Happiness'* by Chris Gardner. When he hit rock bottom, we were all rooting for his success. What about Pastor Paula White who suffered years of sexual and physical abuse at the hands of multiple people after her dad whom she adored committed suicide? Even Michael Jackson, who could arguably be considered the most gifted entertainer in the world, suffered years of physical and emotional abuse growing up.

All these people are notable celebrities whom we have watched throughout the years. We've sympathized with their struggles while rooting for their success. However, you don't have to turn on the television to find people who have overcome the odds against them. All of us know someone who was lost, rejected and had little, or no family support growing up. For those people, it seemed like the cards were stacked against them so high that they were destined for failure.

They were the ones for whom you had no expectations because there didn't seem to be anything positive in their future.

At the same time, you may have watched a neighbor grow up who'd lost her mom, had and absentee dad and was raised by a grandma who was so old that the girl really had to raise herself. Grandma merely provided shelter for the young girl, who because she was the oldest, had to care for her siblings when she herself still needed a parent.

One driving factor that compelled me to continue to press forward was rooted in fear. Now I know that does not sound encouraging at all. However, it is a part of my truth. It gripped me, made me move when I wanted to give up on myself and life overall. A major moment was when I had to deal with the death of my mother. I did not want to focus on my dreams, I did not want to envision light at the end of the tunnel. Candidly speaking, there was so much being thrown at my siblings and me at the time, that we could barely process her rapid regression and untimely death.

My fear has always been that there is no one to catch me if I fall. I cannot afford to fail. Here's the beautiful thing. It isn't my reality, but it is my truth. Based on childhood traumatic experiences, I have been my own primary caregiver since I was a teenager. I did not rely upon others to survive. That protection barrier helped me to press forward, but also served as a hindrance when seeking to develop fruitful relationships. No one wants to engage in long term relationships with people who give off the aura that they don't need anyone. The reality is that I have siblings who will always have my back and an immediate family that loves me dearly. I am never alone.

I share this because the pursuit of dreams require honest

reflection of what potential areas of vulnerability lies ahead. To think obstacles will not emerge, or storms are avoidable is disingenuous at best. However, if you are aware of your areas of weakness, you can heavily rely upon your Wiz team to help you navigate through that rough terrain.

Although sad, the above scenarios can have a bright ending. As the years creep by, some people find themselves still standing, doing well in school and maintaining a positive outlook on life. These are the people who when they are accepted into college, and later graduate and get a good job, you cheer and celebrate their success as if it were your own.

What do these people have in common with celebrities? They all worked hard and refused to accept mediocrity. The young college graduate is just as successful as the professional athlete making millions because they both took the hand they were dealt and learned to make lemonade out of the lemons in their life. If you are committed to becoming successful, you will. Just know that it will require hard work, diligence and the right attitude. I know too many people who are naturally gifted and have the ability to make their dreams come true but aren't willing to work hard. Unfortunately, reliance on talent exclusively is simply not enough. There will always be someone more beautiful, smarter and gifted than you. What will separate you from them is your willingness to go the extra mile and do whatever it takes to achieve your goals.

When I released Dare to Dream in January 2010, the words nestled in these pages were the sentiments of my heart, but they were also aspirational. During that season of my life, I was seeking to find balance and take that challenge by God head on. He said my dreams didn't impress Him? Well then let's partner to figure out who I am and what I am supposed to accomplish in this world. What a difference a decade makes. In different areas of my life, I was fortunate to make significant strides toward my dreams. Let's begin with my educational journey. I graduated from Oral Roberts University in December 2013 with honors. Just prior to graduation, I knew the end game was to complete doctoral studies in some area that focused on prison reformation. I enrolled into a Master of Divinity program in January 2014 and completed my studies in May 2016, again with honors. In January 2017, I walked through the doors of Boston University to begin my doctoral studies. In December 2019, I successfully defended my project and became Rev. Dr. Nicole B. Simpson, CFP®. It still feels surreal.

I am very excited for you because I know that every moment you spend working on your dreams moves you one step closer to peace in every area of your life and motivates you to believe that dreams really do come true!

DREAM ON PURPOSE

I realized a long time ago that there is a connection between my vocation and my purpose. My ability to manage people's money is a gift that has led to my success in the financial services industry. It drives me to work hard and be the best. My motivation is predicated on my fundamental belief that if money were not an issue, we as a society would be free to serve each other in such a powerful and intimate way—a way that empowers and enables us to grow.

I discovered my purpose in the midst of fulfilling my dreams. When I took control of my life, I noticed that my strengths were intertwined. My experience in overcoming sexual assault, being a teenage parent who squandered opportunity and suffering emotionally as a survivor of the World Trade Center attacks all prepared me to assist others in recovering from catastrophic and traumatic events in their own lives.

It isn't easy to pick up the pieces of your life after dangling on the edge of devastation. It takes strength and it takes courage. It also requires following the examples of others who have excelled despite the obstacles they faced. Just knowing that someone else knows how you feel and what you're going through but managed to persevere in spite of serves as an encouragement to the fact that you too can make it.

It's very important to remember that no matter what you're going through, somebody is watching and depending on you to excel. Like it, or not, you are a major influence in someone's life and there is nothing you can do to change that. You have no control over who you influence, but you can control the message you portray!

At this point you may be wondering why you're still here. I personally don't know your answer, but I can assure you that you have work to do. Your life's purpose has not yet been fulfilled; you still have something to accomplish. So, the question should not be why, but rather what do I need to do now?

As I wrote this book, I dreamed that the information presented would awaken your dream and uproot and set you free from the deep-seated insecurities, excuses and roadblocks that have hindered you in times past. With all the challenges we face from day to day as a society, we cannot afford to stop dreaming.
This world needs people who are willing to dream of things that don't yet exist. This world needs you!

For many, dreaming may seem unrealistic, but it truly defines the core of your existence. It is your dreams that position you to reach for the stars, stretch beyond yourself and encourage someone else.

You are never too old to set another goal, or dream a new dream.

C.S. Lewis

EPILOGUE

As I reflect on my personal dreams, I want you to know and understand that I wrote this book at a season in my life where many of my dreams did not yet materialize. I was thick in the midst of the work, work, work stage, working with the stated objective of dreaming on purpose.

Ten years later, I am dreaming new dreams because hard work legitimately pays off. Each decade has presented unique universal challenges that complicate the best laid out plans for our futures. I have learned how important it is to remain willing to adapt. For me, my World Trade Center survival experience altered the course of my life forever. However, while my dreams were on life support, they did not die.

When I released the book originally, I made up in my mind that I would achieve certain measurable goals. Throughout my journey, I never specifically stated what I believe my life purpose is. So here goes...I have been anointed to help people recover from traumatic experiences spiritually, mentally, emotionally, and economically. It took me the last decade to clearly articulate my purpose in this world. It took that same time for me to get the appropriate credentials, establish relationships, build up credibility and do the work to become a trusted ally for those seeking guidance.

This decade, the year of 2020 came in with most people feeling pretty optimistic about their future. Things in society at large have been relatively progressive, leaving people to chart the course of their lives. Hope abounded and people legitimately anticipated this would be a great decade. Then the world stood still. I want to simply remind everyone to remain adaptable. Be willing to shift, slightly deviate from the methodology of your plan to achieve your dreams. I have learned that you can travel many roads to get to a stated designation. Do not change your dreams, just commit to taking an alternative route.

I know firsthand that my past successes came with a significant price, but that price has already been paid; now it's up to me to dare to dream. So, I am moving forward. I wrote my dream about the Wheel of Fortune in this book because I felt that something was missing. What hit home for me was that I could not compete because I did not make myself available. I believe I am qualified for the position, so what was my fear?

I've changed that in my own life. After completing this book, I searched out the rules and conditions to become a contestant on the show. I am moving forward confident that I can do all things. They're going to have to reject me because I refuse to take myself out of contention for anything else in life. Are you with me? Are you willing to dare to dream?

BEGIN YOUR LIFE JOURNEY WITH "THE "ULTIMATE PLAN"

Reverend Dr. Nicole B. Simpson, CFP® is a practitioner with over 29 years of experience in the securities industry. On September 11, 2001, her life was drastically altered as a financial planner working at 2 World Trade Center on the 73rd floor. Simpson was still in the building on the 44th floor when Tower 2 was hit during the World Trade Center attacks.

Today, Simpson compassionately assists families on how to begin to walk along the road to recovery when faced with a catastrophic, unexpected disaster. She is actively involved in spiritual, emotional and economic empowerment. A compelling empowerment speaker, television/ radio personality and author, Ms. Simpson travels throughout the United States teaching in a practical and easy to understand manner. Her simple approach motivates everyone who hears her message to take action to change their future. Her commitment is to engage people with the thought, "If money were not an issue, what would be your life's purpose?"

Pastor Nicole's life began to take shape when she turned seven years old. Gifted with a bible by her mom she spent most her time in her room reading the red words in that Bible, sparking her interest.

Those red words told her to do good to please God and it taught her how to pray. It was through scripture, she learned how to seek God's comfort in the midst of every storm. Like most individuals, she has suffered unexpected, significant personal tragedy that affected her entire family emotionally and financially. What is critical, but often avoided, is the experience and willingness to share strategies that instruct others how to overcome unexpected disasters that can stagnate one's personal life because of a crisis. "How does one pick up the pieces of their life and move toward their ordained purpose?" She can answer those questions and put into perspective the necessary steps to begin the recovery process.

She is the visionary and CEO of the Power of Gospel Ministries and an entrepreneur. In January 2016, she embarked on a new life journey becoming the Pastor of Micah 7 Ministries located in Piscataway, NJ. Simpson has authored several books; Planning for A Reason, a Season, and a Lifetime, The Ultimate Plan...A Financial Survival Guide for Life's Unexpected Events which was nationally distributed through Tate Publishing and Dare 2 Dream...Pushing Past Your Pain to Pursue Purpose, a book that changes the lives of everyone who reads it. It later became her first Amazon best seller. In June 2011, she released 9/11/01 A Long Road Toward Recovery, her second best-selling book. The book reflected upon the challenges of World Trade Center survivors who were neglected emotionally and economically. In January 2014, she released her fifth book titled Personal Prayer for all Occasions and her highly anticipated sixth title addressing how to recognize the voice of God has been recently released: Listen and Learn How God Speaks to You. Her media profile includes appearances on CNN News, BBC World News, Huffington

Post, Crains NY Business, Fox News and UPN

9. Simpson is a Cum Laude graduate of Oral Roberts University. She completed her Masters of Divinity degree at New Brunswick Theological Seminary in May 2016 Magna Cum Laude. In January 2017, Simpson enrolled into Boston University to purse her Doctorate of Ministries in Transformational Leadership and completed the program in December 2019.

Ms. Simpson has authored 6 books which can be purchased on Amazon.com:

https://www.amazon.com/Nicole-B-Simpson/e/B00345M1UK/ref=dp_byline_cont_all_1

| Personal Prayer for all occasions | Listen and Learn How God Speaks to You | The Ultimate Plan: A Financial Survival Guide for Life's Unexpected Events | Planning for A Reason, A Season, & A Lifetime | 09/11/01 A Long Road Toward Recovery | Dare 2 Dream Pushing Past Your Pain to Pursue Purpose |

For further information about the life and ministry of Nicole B. Simpson or to inquire about her speaking schedule, contact Harvest Wealth LLC at 732-377-2024.